FUNDAMENTALS

BEST KARATE 2

Fundamentals

M. Nakayama

KODANSHA INTERNATIONAL LTD.

Tokyo, New York & San Francisco

Photo credits: p. 14, bottom, from *Golf*, published by Kodansha Ltd.; p. 61, Kendō photos from *Kendō*, published by Kodansha Ltd.; front cover photo and p. 61 Nō photo by Keizō Kaneko.

Distributors: United States: Kodansha International / USA, Ltd. through Harper & Row, Publishers, Inc., 10 East 53rd Street, New York, New York 10022. South America: Harper & Row, International Department. Canada: Fitzhenry & Whiteside Limited, 150 Lesmill Road, Don Mills, Ontario. Mexico and Central America: Harla S.A. de C.V., Apartado 30–546, Mexico 4, D.F. Europe: Boxerbooks, Inc., Limmatstrasse 111, 8031 Zurich. The Far East: Toppan Company (S) Pte. Ltd., Box 22 Jurong Town Post Office, Jurong, Singapore 22.

Published by Kodansha International Ltd., 2–12–21 Otowa, Bunkyo-ku, Tokyo 112 and Kodansha International / USA, Ltd., 10 East 53rd Street, New York, New York 10022 and 44 Montgomery Street, San Francisco, California 94104. Copyright © 1978 by Kodansha International Ltd.
All rights reserved. Printed in Japan.

LCC 77–74829
ISBN 0–87011–324–0
JBC 2375–786423–2361

First edition, 1978

CONTENTS

Dedicated
to my teacher
GICHIN FUNAKOSHI

INTRODUCTION

The past decade has seen a great increase in the popularity of karate-dō throughout the world. Among those who have been attracted to it are college students and teachers, artists, businessmen and civil servants. It has come to be practiced by policemen and members of Japan's Self-defense Forces. In a number of universities, it has become a compulsory subject, and that number is increasing yearly.

Along with the increase in popularity, there have been certain unfortunate and regrettable interpretations and performances. For one thing, karate has been confused with the so-called Chinese-style boxing, and its relationship with the original Okinawan *Te* has not been sufficiently understood. There are also people who have regarded it as a mere show, in which two men attack each other savagely, or the contestants battle each other as though it were a form of boxing in which the feet are used, or a man shows off by breaking bricks or other hard objects with his head, hand or foot.

If karate is practiced solely as a fighting technique, this is cause for regret. The fundamental techniques have been developed and perfected through long years of study and practice, but to make any effective use of these techniques, the spiritual aspect of this art of self-defense must be recognized and must play the predominant role. It is gratifying to me to see that there are those who understand this, who know that karate-dō is a purely Oriental martial art, and who train with the proper attitude.

To be capable of inflicting devastating damage on an opponent with one blow of the fist or a single kick has indeed been the objective of this ancient Okinawan martial art. But even the practitioners of old placed stronger emphasis on the spiritual side of the art than on the techniques. Training means training of body and spirit, and, above all else, one should treat his opponent courteously and with the proper etiquette. It is not enough to fight with all one's power; the real objective in karate-dō is to do so for the sake of justice.

Gichin Funakoshi, a great master of karate-dō, pointed out repeatedly that the first purpose in pursuing this art is the nurturing of a sublime spirit, a spirit of humility. Simultaneously, power sufficient to destroy a ferocious wild animal with a single blow should be developed. Becoming a true follower of karate-dō is possible only when one attains perfection in these two aspects, the one spiritual, the other physical.

Karate as an art of self-defense and karate as a means of improving and maintaining health has long existed. During the past twenty years, a new activity has been explored and is coming to the fore. This is *sports karate.*

In sports karate, contests are held for the purpose of determining the ability of the participants. This needs emphasizing, for here again there is cause for regret. There is a tendency to place too much emphasis on winning contests, and those who do so neglect the practice of fundamental techniques, opting instead to attempt jiyū kumite at the earliest opportunity.

Emphasis on winning contests cannot help but alter the fundamental techniques a person uses and the practice he engages in. Not only that, it will result in a person's being incapable of executing a strong and effective technique, which, after all, is the unique characteristic of karate-dō. The man who begins jiyū kumite prematurely—without having practiced fundamentals sufficiently—will soon be overtaken by the man who has trained in the basic techniques long and diligently. It is, quite simply, a matter of haste makes waste. There is no alternative to learning and practicing basic techniques and movements step by step, stage by stage.

If karate competitions are to be held, they must be conducted under suitable conditions and in the proper spirit. The desire to win a contest is counterproductive, since it leads to a lack of seriousness in learning the fundamentals. Moreover, aiming for a savage display of strength and power in a contest is totally undesirable. When this happens, courtesy toward the opponent is forgotten, and this is of prime importance in any expression of karate. I believe this matter deserves a great deal of reflection and self-examination by both instructors and students.

To explain the many and complex movements of the body, it has been my desire to present a fully illustrated book with an up-to-date text, based on the experience in this art that I have acquired over a period of forty-six years. This hope is being realized by the publication of the *Best Karate* series, in which earlier writings of mine have been totally revised with the help and encouragement of my readers. This new series explains in detail what karate-dō is in language made as simple as possible, and I sincerely hope that it will be of help to followers of karate-dō. I hope also that karateka in many countries will be able to understand each other better through this series of books.

Deciding who is the winner and who is the loser is not the ultimate objective. Karate-dō is a martial art for the development of character through training, so that the karateka can surmount any obstacle, tangible or intangible.

Karate-dō is an empty-handed art of self-defense in which the arms and legs are systematically trained and an enemy attacking by surprise can be controlled by a demonstration of strength like that of using actual weapons.

Karate-dō is exercise through which the karateka masters all body movements, such as bending, jumping and balancing, by learning to move limbs and body backward and forward, left and right, up and down, freely and uniformly.

The techniques of karate-dō are well controlled according to the karateka's will power and are directed at the target accurately and spontaneously.

The essence of karate techniques is *kime*. The meaning of *kime* is an explosive attack to the target using the appropriate technique and maximum power in the shortest time possible. (Long ago, there was the expression *ikken hissatsu*, meaning "to kill with one blow," but to assume from this that killing is the objective is dangerous and incorrect. It should be remembered that the karateka of old were able to practice *kime* daily and in dead seriousness by using the makiwara.)

Kime may be accomplished by striking, punching or kicking, but also by blocking. A technique lacking *kime* can never be regarded as true karate, no matter how great the resemblance to karate. A contest is no exception; however, it is against the rules to make contact because of the danger involved.

Sun-dome means to arrest a technique just before contact with the target (one *sun*, about three centimeters). But not carrying a technique through to *kime* is not true karate, so the question is how to reconcile the contradiction between *kime* and *sun-dome*. The answer is this: establish the target slightly in front of the opponent's vital point. It can then be hit in a controlled way with maximum power, without making contact.

Training transforms various parts of the body into weapons to be used freely and effectively. The quality necessary to accomplish this is self-control. To become a victor, one must first overcome his own self.

English team, Tokyo, 1977

American Bicentennial Matches, 1976

THE SOURCE OF POWER

In the decisive techniques (*kime-waza*) of karate is hidden a tremendous, explosive power. This power is produced by the movements of the body; especially important is the turning of the upper body in conjunction with the rotation of the hips. Turning the hips smoothly and rapidly, while keeping them level, is found in other sports too, such as pitching and hitting in baseball, driving in golf, and in the shotput. But neither in other sports nor in the punching and striking of karate is the extension and contraction of the arm alone sufficient to produce an effective technique.

In karate, *block with the hips, punch with the hips.*

The beauty of the traditional Japanese dance depends on the hips. (Chōjirō Hananoe, Teacher of the Hananoe-ryū)

The swing of golf champion Takashi Murakami. Ideal form.

1. Starting with orders from the brain,
2. the *hiki-te* acts like an automobile starter,
3. the hips begin to rotate,
4. at the same time the torso turns smoothly,
5. and the punching arm connects solidly
   with the target.

The swing of homerun record holder Sadaharu Oh. Smooth rotation centered on the hips.

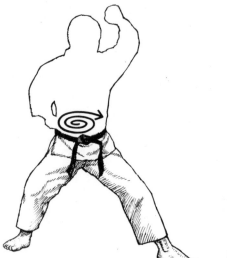

Jōdan age-uke. Winding the spring.

Gyaku-zuki. Letting the spring unwind.

Rotating the Hips

A technique cannot be sharp and decisive unless the rotation of the hips is utilized to the fullest.

Basically, training in rotation of the hips begins with fast movement on a fairly large scale. As one advances in skill, the rotation should be fast but on a small scale. Eventually the feeling should be one of the hips turning in a sharp cutting movement.

As for techniques, there are those with a fast, strong, large movement and those with a rapid, sharp, small movement. It is essential to learn which technique is appropriate to which situation. This can only be done by accumulating practice.

Important in beginning training is the mastery of large-scale technique that is fast, strong, up to the standard and that travels the correct route.

The faster the rotation of the hips, the better, for this gives an abundance of speed to the technique. The principle of the rotation is the same as that of a spring. The tighter the spring is wound, the greater will be the force when it is released. Rotating the hips (to the half-front-facing position) and blocking is like winding the spring. Rotating the hips the other way (to the original position) and punching is like releasing the spring.

Withdrawing arm (hiki-te)—*Hip rotation* (*block*)—*Reverse hip rotation—Punch*

16

Relation between withdrawing hand and hip rotation

Without changing position, hips and shoulders turn at the same time.

The Important Points

1. Keep the hips horizontal to the floor, and rotate them smoothly.

2. Do not allow either hip to raise; always keep them level.

3. Do not turn the shoulders only. Turn the upper body smoothly and in unison with the hips.

4. Always keep the torso upright, taking care that the buttocks do not protrude to the rear.

Practice Methods

Order of practice: Preparatory position—Half-front-facing position—Front-facing position—Half-front-facing position

1. *Preparatory position.* Facing to the front in the front stance (*zenkutsu-dachi*), place both palms on the hips. With the thumbs, press the hipbones upward. Keep the torso erect.

2. *Half-front-facing position.* In the front stance, rotate the hips strongly to one side (*hanmi,* 45° from the front-facing position). The turning of the upper body must be coordinated with the turning of the hips.

3. *Front-facing position.* Keeping the upper body straight, rotate the hips smoothly and evenly to face the front. Just at the end of this movement, power is most substantial. At this instant, thrust vigorously downward with the back leg.

4. *Half-front-facing position.* Removing all power, silently and slowly return to the half-front-facing position.

Successive Rotation

When techniques are executed, as in blocking and then punching or punching, blocking and then punching again, the hips must be rotated successively. In shifting from the front facing, to half-front-facing, to front facing, to half-front-facing position, if the spring is wound fully, then the unwinding will be most natural and correct. To make fullest use of the hips, the muscles in the side of the abdomen must be fully tensed. Only with maximum tension of these muscles will the hips rotate naturally.

Reverse punch

Regular and Reverse Rotation

According to the technique, the rotation of the hips is regular or reverse. There is no difference in the effectiveness of the technique.

Jun Kaiten   Regular Rotation

The direction of rotation and the direction of the technique are the same.

Hips rotate to the left; right fist is used for such techniques as straight punch (*choku-zuki*), roundhouse punch (*mawashi-zuki*) and hook punch (*kagi-zuki*). Hips rotate to the right; left arm is used for such techniques as rising block (*age-uke*) and blocking from outside inward (*soto-uke*).

Rising block

Left jab

Left block,
outside inward

Downward block

Gyaku Kaiten   *Reverse Rotation*

The direction of rotation and the direction of the technique are on opposite sides. Hips rotate to the right; technique is executed to the left.

In principal, reverse rotation is used for the downward block (*gedan barai*); blocking against body attack, inside outward (*chūdan uchi-uke*); sword hand block (*shutō uke*) and so on. In sparring, however, there are cases, as when one is at very close quarters, when these blocks may be performed with regular rotation.

Block against body attack, inside outward

Sword hand block

23

Hanmi   Half-front-facing Position

The hip of the forward leg is in front. There is a tendency for the forward hip to draw backward and the upper body to lean forward (e.g., when making a left block from outside inward with the bottom of the wrist). To avoid this, the feeling should be that of pushing the hip upward.

Gyaku Hanmi   Reverse Half-front-facing Position

The hip of the rear leg is to the front. Because the legs are turned fully inward, the stance is somewhat narrower than in the *hanmi*. It is important to have the feeling of thrusting the hip that executes the technique forward to the fullest extent (e.g., the right hip in a right block from inside outward).

24

Half-front-facing position

Reverse half-front-facing position

Raising the left hip to the front

Raising the right hip to the front

No less important in the generation of power than hip rotation is the thrusting forward of the hips. In making a positive and vigorous attack, one that prevents the opponent from counterattacking, aptitude in thrusting the hips forward is a crucial point between success and failure.

In this movement, the front leg is the supporting leg. The rear leg, and thus the upper body, is brought up to the front leg. At this point, the supporting leg is thrust backward and downward with great force. This pushes the hips and body forward.

This is not the same as stepping forward. Motive power comes from the powerful thrust of the supporting leg; the principle is the same as that of the jet engine. The bulk of the body weight is directly over the hips, which carry the body forward. The vital core of the movement is the reaction between the supporting leg and the floor. The greater this reaction is, the faster the body advances.

The route power travels is from the hips to the spine to the shoulders to the arms. For the transmission of power to be smooth, the hips and pelvis must be firmly connected with the spine and upper body. At the same time that the muscles of the abdomen are tensed, those supporting the spine must also be tensed. If the abdominal muscles are not sufficiently tensed, the hips and torso will be flaccid. As a result, the power of the hips cannot be properly channeled, and the punch or strike will be weak.

Whether in the lunge punch or other techniques, uniting and fully applying the power of rotation and the power of the forward movement maximizes momentum and makes for a very powerful and effective technique. How this works can be seen by taking a back stance diagonally to the rear. If the front leg is then driven forcefully against the floor, the hips and body will move diagonally backward.

In the front stance, when the supporting foot is thrust downward, the gluteus maximus muscles move the hip joints, the quadriceps the knee joints, and the gastrocnemius and soleus muscles the ankle joints. It is very worthwhile learning the correlation between muscles and movements, so that the muscles can be used specifically.

1. When advancing, the center of gravity moves forward, and the body weight comes to the supporting leg. Though the knee of this leg is bent, the leg must be kept strong and flexible.

2. The back leg and the torso are drawn in unison to the supporting leg.

3. The entire sole of the supporting foot should be in firm contact with the floor. The other foot should move with a lightly floating feeling and lightly touch the supporting foot.

4. When the supporting leg is straightened, thrust it diagonally backward and downward with a strong kicklike feeling. Use the reaction to move the hips forward rapidly. At the same time, advance one step with the other foot.

5. The other leg slides well forward into the front stance. When it stops, tense all the muscles of the thigh and calf for an instant. (This leg becomes the important supporting leg for the next technique.)

6. The foot slides lightly, as though there were a thin piece of paper between it and the floor, and describes a shallow arc to the inner side.

7. Neither the height of the hips nor the direction in which the center of gravity is moving should be changed during the movement. If the hips move up or down, the direction of power becomes uncertain and stability is lost.

8. To be prepared for any change in the situation, it is necessary to keep power firmly in the abdomen and keep the upper body directly over the hips and vertically straight.

Correct form

Incorrect form

Training Methods

1. While in the informal attention stance (*heisoku-dachi*), place both palms on the hips, thumbs toward the spine. Elbows out to the sides, shoulders relaxed, chest out, lower abdomen fairly tense, have the feeling of pushing the pelvis forward with the thumbs. As much as possible, keep the knees flexible.

2. Straightening the left knee, thrust the leg diagonally to the rear, sole firmly in contact with the floor. At the same time, put power in the palms and push the pelvis fully forward.

3. Also at the same time, slide the right foot lightly one step forward.

4. With the right knee fully bent, take a right front stance.

5. Bring the right foot back to its original position and assume the informal attention stance.

6. Sliding the left foot, advance one step.

7. Practice by repeating the above movements.

Thrusting hips forward from informal attention stance

Upper body leaning forward

When facing to the front, correct this by pushing the hipbones upward and forward, making use especially of the thumbs. In the half-facing position, the forward hip may pull back and the torso fall forward. Correct this by trying to push the bones of the rear hip upward and forward.

Shoulders turning before the hips

By tightening the lower abdomen, especially the muscles directly concerned and those on the sides, the pelvis and chest can be strongly joined together. They will be like a single board, and hips and shoulders will turn at the same time.

Back heel floating

If the knee of the rear leg sinks and the heel rises, it will interfere with rotating the hips fully. While flexing the knee fully, straighten the leg to keep the heel from floating.

If too much body weight is on the front leg, the rear heel will float. Then you can be easily upset by an opponent sweeping your leg out from under you. The important point is to have the entire sole in contact with the floor and to press down strongly.

Hips not on a level keel

It is not uncommon to see the hips out of position or moving up or down. The legs must be strong and the knees and ankles taut and unmoving. Special care should be taken that the front knee does not move.

Supporting leg not strong; shoulders leading the body

In either case, stability of the lower body will be poor, causing techniques to be weak. The ankle must be strong and taut, the knee straightened fully, and the hips thrust forward strongly.

Only legs moving forward

Mistiming of the movement of the torso will result in a technique that is indecisive and weak in effect. Torso, legs, hips and punch must move at the same time. Move the hips as rapidly as possible. You must have the intention of executing a decisive technique.

Photos on opposite page show *incorrect* form.

Columbian team, Los Angeles, 1975

Trinidad-Tobago team, Los Angeles, 1975

DEVELOPING GOOD STANCE

The Importance of Correct Stance

A strong technique is born from a firm, sure-footed stance. Whether the technique is offensive or defensive, it will not be effective if the body lacks balance and stability. The ability to counter an attack under any circumstances depends largely on the maintenance of correct form. For techniques to be powerful, fast, accurate and smoothly executed, they must be launched from a strong and stable base.

In karate, *stance* (*tachikata*) refers to the position of the lower body, the hips and the legs, which literally carry the upper body. Thus techniques are at their best when form is at the optimum. The moment when this is important is the instant in which a technique is executed. Good form is not rigid. Over-concentration on maintaining a firm and stable position will result in loss of mobility, which is necessary for the succeeding movement.

It is well to remember that skyscrapers can be built only on a solid foundation.

Requirements of Good Stance

The basis of executing a technique is correct stance plus balance and the harmonious coordination of all parts of the body. Both feet, both legs, the torso, both arms and both hands must be well controlled, and all must work together at the same time. In this way, techniques become fast and powerful. The delicate control that is required depends on and is guided by good stance.

When executing a technique:

1. Be well balanced.
2. Rotate the hips smoothly.
3. Use maximum speed.
4. Be sure that power is sufficient and control is easily managed.
5. Be sure that the muscles appropriate to the particular technique move smoothly and that the muscle groups work in harmonious cooperation. For this reason, learn *which* muscles are used *when*. (See pages 136–9.)

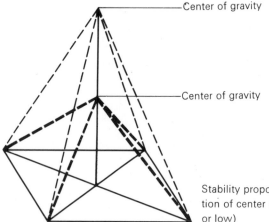

Center of gravity

Center of gravity

Stability proportional to location of center of gravity (high or low)

Stance and Stability

Stability is in direct proportion to the area encompassed by the feet. For example, the back stance has a higher degree of stability than the cat leg stance, while the front stance is more stable than the back stance.

The height of the center of gravity is also a factor. The lower the center of gravity, the more stable the stance.

To absorb the reaction that occurs when a technique is strongly executed, the posture must be low and the stance must be one in which the feet encompass a large area. The stance must be strong but flexible.

Considering strength and stability, the best stance comes from having the soles of both feet solidly on the floor and bracing the legs by twisting the thighs firmly toward each other. Thus the rooted stance, front stance, straddle-leg stance and square stance have a high degree of stability.

A stance in which the area encompassed by the feet is not great can also be stable, however. The hourglass stance, for example, has greater stability than either the back stance or the cat leg stance.

Special stances, such as standing on only the left leg, or having the support of only one leg when kicking have a relatively low degree of stability.

After comparing the various stances, one must also learn how to make proper and effective use of each one. And at all times in training, one must keep stability in mind.

For strength and stability, it is necessary to have the feeling that the line connecting the navel and the anus is as short as possible.

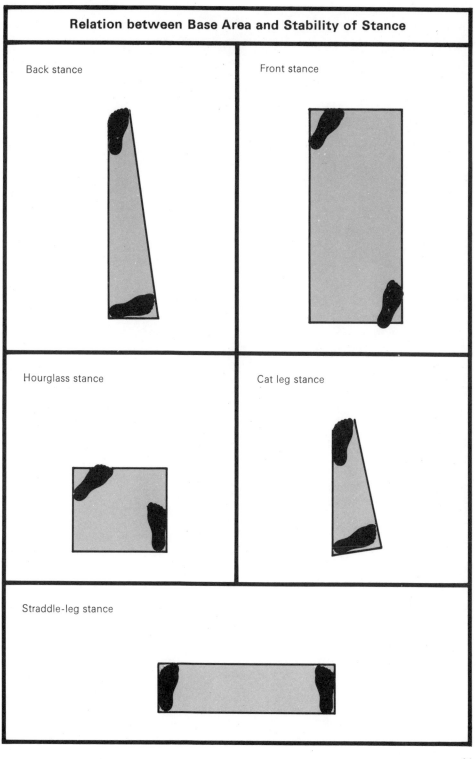

Relation between Base Area and Stability of Stance

Back stance

Front stance

Hourglass stance

Cat leg stance

Straddle-leg stance

Classification of Stances

Stances can be divided into two groups according to the way the knees are used in relation to the center of gravity.

In one group, the knees are pressed strongly outward from the (imaginery) line connecting the body's center of gravity and the floor, as in the straddle-leg stance, rooted stance, front stance, square stance and (back leg only) back stance.

In the other group, the knees are twisted inward, as in the hourglass stance and half-moon stance.

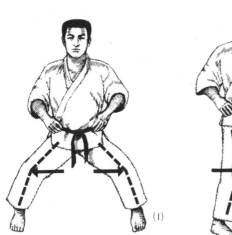

1. Both knees pressed outward

2. Both knees twisted inward

Front stance

Back stance

Straddle-leg stance

Rooted stance

The Important Points

Spreading the Knees

Imagine a line connecting the knees and extending on outward to the sides. Spread the knees strongly outward on the extended line. (Straddle-leg, rooted and front stances.)

Front stance

Cat leg stance

Back stance

Square stance

Knees and Toes

Whatever the stance, the knees and toes of each leg should point in the same direction.

Knees and Ankles

Knees and ankles must be bent sufficiently and strongly locked.

Feet attached to the floor as if they had suction cups

Soles

The entire surface of the soles should be in reliable contact with the floor. The feeling is that of strong adhesion.

Height of the Hips

Whatever the stance, the height of the hips does not vary significantly.

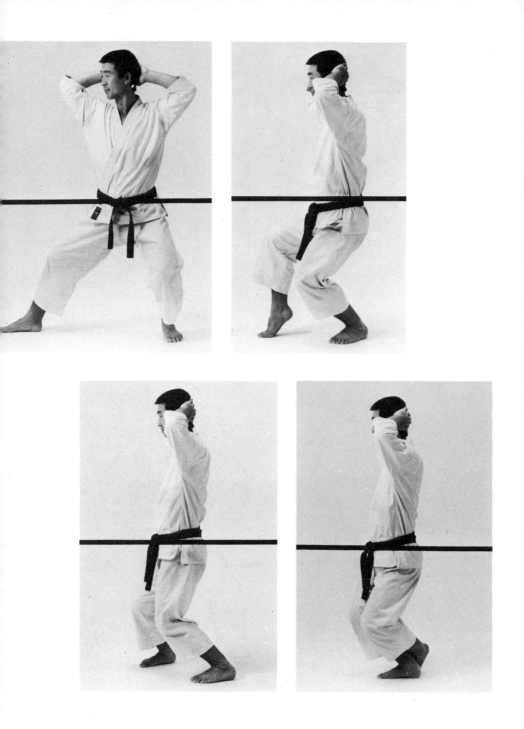

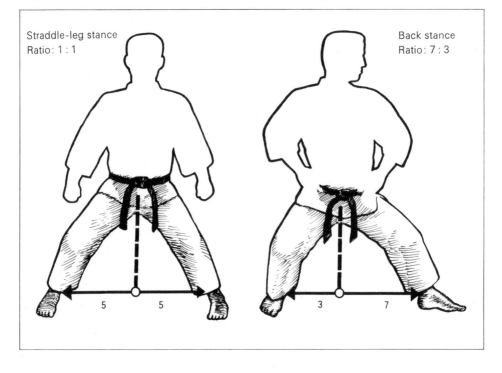

Straddle-leg stance
Ratio: 1 : 1

5   5

Back stance
Ratio: 7 : 3

3   7

Position of the Hips

According to the stance, the position of the hips must be accurately differentiated.

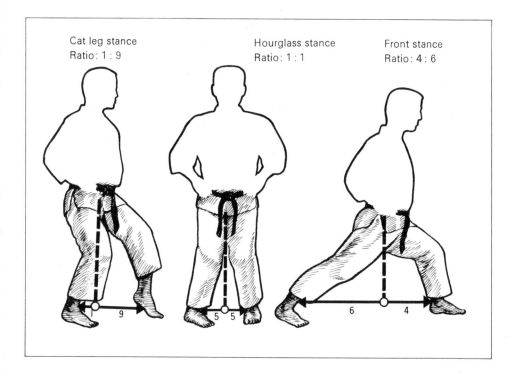

Cat leg stance
Ratio: 1 : 9

Hourglass stance
Ratio: 1 : 1

Front stance
Ratio: 4 : 6

Zenkutsu-dachi

Stance and Technique

Stances vary according to objective.

Zenkutsu-dachi   Front Stance

This is used when power is to be directed to the front.

Kiba-dachi   Straddle-leg Stance

This can be used when attacks come from both sides.

Kōkutsu-dachi   Back Stance
Neko-ashi-dachi   Cat Leg Stance

These are useful for blocking when moving backward, or for getting the body safely out of the opponent's range.

Kōsa-dachi   Crossed-feet Stance

Uses of this stance include jumping in very close to the opponent and landing after a high jump. When landing, the body weight should be placed on one leg, rather than both legs.

To be able to maintain good balance while standing on one leg, the other leg crosses behind the heel or in front of the ankle of the supporting leg.

Kiba-dachi

Neko-ashi-dachi

Kōsa-dachi

Training Methods

1. Start from the natural position (*shizen-tai*).

2. Sliding the left foot one step forward, take the left front stance.

3. Bring the left foot back; take the natural position.

4. Sliding the right foot one step forward, take the right front stance.

5. Bring the right foot back; take the natural position.

6. Sliding the left foot one step to the side, take the straddle-leg stance.

7. Bring the left foot back; take the natural position.

8. Sliding the right foot one step to the side, take the straddle-leg stance.

9. Bring the right foot back; take the natural position.

10. Drawing the left foot one step backward, take the left back stance.

11. Bring the left foot back; take the natural position.

12. Drawing the right foot one step backward, take the right back stance.

13. Bring the right foot back; take the natural position.

14. Drawing the right foot one step backward, take the left front stance.

15. Bring the right foot back; take the natural position.

16. Drawing the left foot one step backward, take the right front stance.

17. Bring the left foot back; take the natural position.

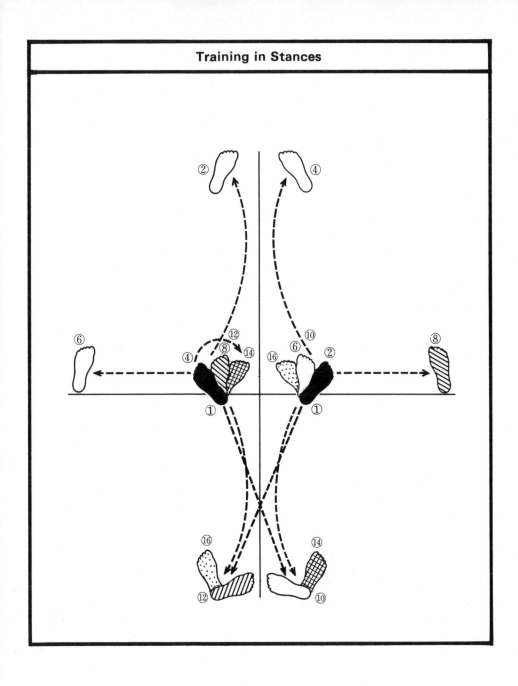

Buttocks sticking out to the rear

While the center of gravity must be low, letting the buttocks protrude to the rear will result in bending the back and losing balance.

Too much concern about form

If you are obsessed about having good form (*katachi*), it will be impossible to have really good stance. Take care to fully tense the inner thigh muscles.

Hips out of place

As mentioned previously, the hips must be kept on the same level. Take care that the bent knee is not relaxed.

Ankles too relaxed

The ankle though bent must be firm; otherwise the stance will be weak.

Heels floating

If the heels are not squarely on the floor, the stance will be weak and unstable.

Heels and toes out of line

The knee and toes of the same leg must always be pointed in the same direction; otherwise balance will be lost.

Photos below show *incorrect* form.

Egypt, 1977

3
DYNAMICS

MOVING AND CHANGING DIRECTION

Executing a technique while moving forward or backward, or to the right or left, is not a matter of walking or running or hopping about like a frog. Movement in any direction depends on using the legs correctly.

One leg is the pivot leg (*jiku ashi*). This is the leg on the side opposite to the direction of movement, and it supplies the starting force. With the forceful straightening of the knee, the foot is driven against the floor, creating a reaction. The hips and upper body then move forward together with the other leg.

The foot of the moving leg (*dō-kyaku*) slides over the floor lightly.

When advancing, the rear leg is the pivot leg. Similarly, when moving to the left, the right leg is the pivot leg.

The differentiation between the pivot leg and the moving leg is an important basic point. It should be learned thoroughly and put into practice. The pivot leg kicks the floor strongly; the moving leg slides very quickly but very smoothly.

In kumite or kata, it is the beginner whose movements are noisy and uneven. The foot of the seasoned karateka will slide lightly, as though there were a single sheet of paper between his foot and the floor. His technique will be strong and sharp, but no matter how intense his movement, he makes no sound, even when landing after a high jump. He skillfully employs *sei* and *dō* (tranquillity and movement, inactivity and activity).

In the case of *fumikomi*, the foot should strike the floor with the feeling that the strength is sufficient to crack a board.

The Nō drama (*suri-ashi*)

Moving Forward

In moving forward, straighten the knee of the pivot foot and strongly and sharply drive the sole, particularly the heel, into the floor. Using the reaction that results from this, thrust the hips forward swiftly, at the same time sliding the other leg forward.

Back stance, moving forward
and backward

Moving Backward

In moving backward from the front stance, the back leg is the pivot leg. Withdraw the hips firmly, as though their weight came to be supported by the heel of the pivot foot, at the same time bringing the foot back in a shallow arc to the inside. The hips turn together into the half-front-facing position.

Because the hips turn especially easily, this is used mostly for blocking.

Front stance

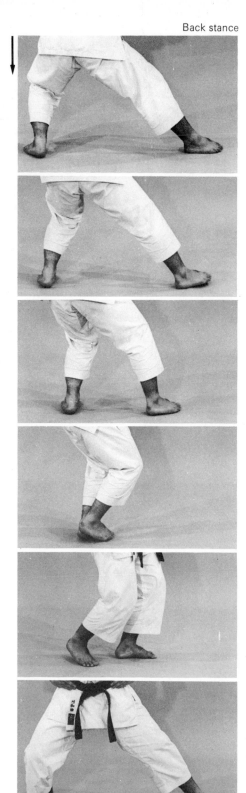

Moving Sideways

The pivot leg is on the side opposite to the direction of movement. Push against the floor strongly and firmly. Use this reaction. The hips and the moving leg go together in the opposite direction.

1

2

Fumidashi

3

4

Fumidashi and Fumikomi

It is important to make a clear distinction between *fumidashi* and *fumikomi*.

Straightening the pivot leg strongly, keeping the hips level and sliding the moving leg lightly—this is *fumidashi*.

Fumikomi is a stamping kick. With the pivot leg as the supporting leg, the other leg is raised high and thrust down forcefully, the entire sole coming into contact with the floor at one time.

Fumikomi

69

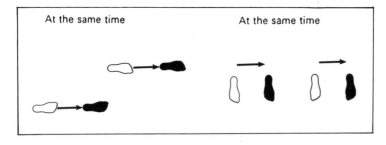

At the same time   At the same time

Yori-ashi   *Sliding the Feet*

Moving both feet at the same time—forward, backward, left or right—without changing the stance or the position of the upper body is known as *yori-ashi*.

The starting force comes from pressing the pivot leg against the floor. Finding an opportunity for movement, the hips, always on an even keel, are thrust to the front, to the back or to one side. Both feet slide lightly and smoothly at the same time. Care must be given to the distance moved. The length of one's own foot is about the limit. Anything greater than this will cause a loss of stability.

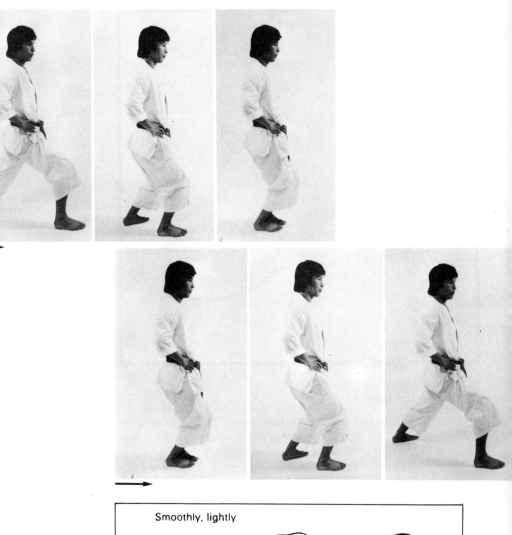

Smoothly, lightly

Changing the Pivot Leg

To change the pivot leg, the foot of the other leg is brought next to the foot of the pivot leg and the body weight immediately shifted from one foot to the other. This is especially useful for shortening the distance between yourself and the opponent.

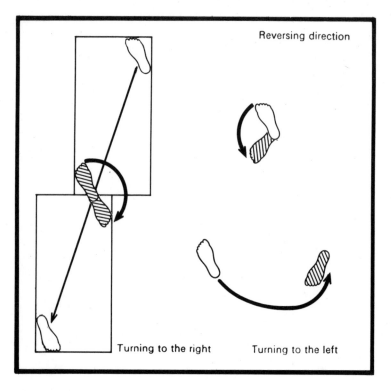

Reversing direction

Turning to the right

Turning to the left

Changing Direction

Changing direction does not mean simply facing in another direction, nor does it mean circling the opponent. Not being able to change direction rapidly will result in a loss of timing.

With the movement centered on the pivot leg, the hips should turn sharply, with a feeling like cutting. The execution of the technique should be simultaneous with the movement. Contact between the sole of the pivot foot and the floor must be firm and sure, the feeling being that the entire sole twists.

Reversing Direction

In reversing direction, the hips are rotated with the feeling of placing the weight on the heel of the pivot foot. This way the rotation will be smooth and the hips can be kept level. If it is not done this way, the hips will float and direction cannot be reversed with sharpness.

Special Method of Changing Direction

The rear foot is brought half a step nearer the hip. Then the head, hip and foot form an imaginary pivot line. Turning like a top, upper body and hips are rotated swiftly, changing the direction one is facing to the side.

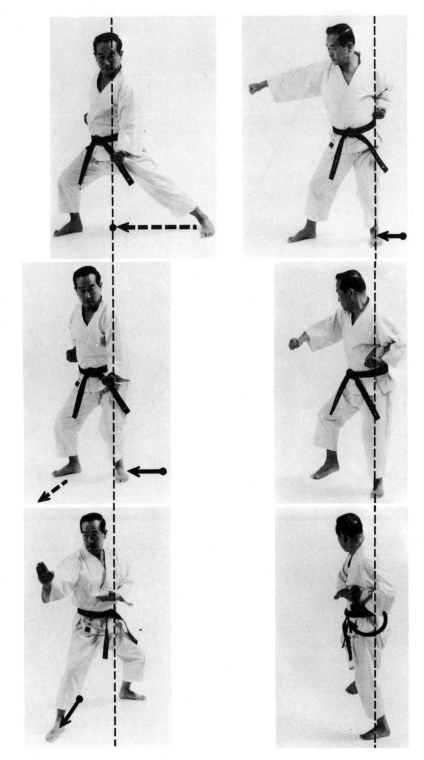

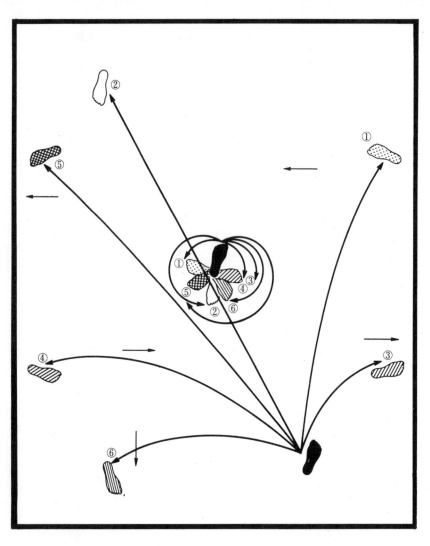

Changing Direction, Training Method A

Left front stance, left leg as pivot leg.

1. Rotate to the left, taking a left front stance to the left side.

2. Rotate widely to the left, taking a left front stance to the rear.

3. Rotate to the right, taking a right front stance to the right side (move the right foot to the right side).

4. Rotate to the right, taking a left front stance to the right side.

5. Rotate widely to the right, taking a right front stance to the left side (sliding the right foot forward, move it to the left side).

6. Rotate to the right, taking a right front stance to the rear (move the right foot to the left side).

74

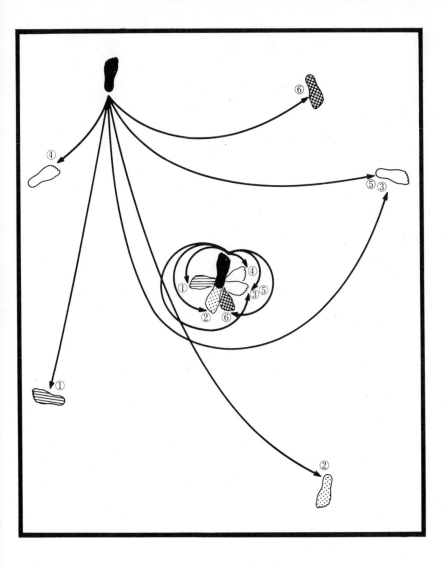

Changing Direction, Training Method B

Left front stance, right leg as pivot leg.

1. Rotate to the left, taking a left front stance to the left side.

2. Rotate to the left, taking a left front stance to the rear.

3. Rotate widely to the left, taking a left front stance to the right side.

4. Rotate to the right, taking a right front stance to the right side (bring the left foot from the rear to the left side).

5. Rotate to the right, taking a left front stance to the right side.

6. Rotate to the right, taking a right front stance to the rear (move the left foot to the right side).

Tai-sabaki

Blocking while handling an opponent's attack, then turning this action into a counterattack is a very important point. Taking care of one's own body and escaping seem at a glance to be very similar, but when they are examined closely, the difference is recognized as being very great.

Escaping, of course, is simply getting far away from an attack, typically without giving a thought to anything else. *Tai-sabaki*, on the other hand, means to handle or manage one's body in such a way as to avoid the attack while at the same time devising a counterattack. For this to be effective, distancing is of great importance. In fact, one should be able to block and counterattack while being at very, very close range.

Thus, circling an opponent is meaningless. What is significant is the ability to make either leg the pivot leg and to turn the hips with a sharp cutting motion.

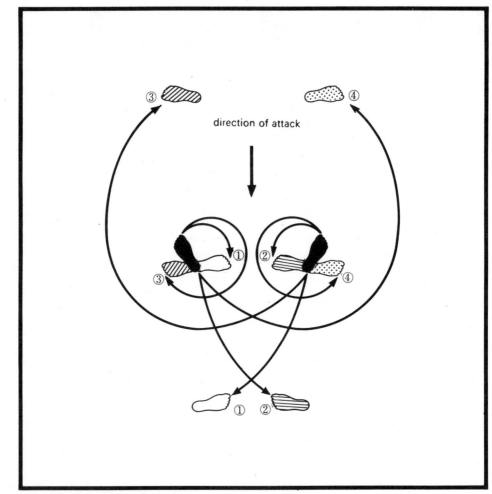

direction of attack

Tai-sabaki, Training Method A

1. Pivoting on the left foot. Rotate hips to the right, bring the right foot to the rear, and face to the right side.

2. Pivoting on the right leg, turn the hips to the left, bring the left foot to the rear, and face to the left side.

3. Pivoting on the left foot, turn the hips to the left, bring the left foot well to the front, and face to the left side.

4. Pivoting on the right leg, turn the hips to the right, bring the left foot well to the front, and face to the right side.

Tai-sabaki, Training Method B

Using essentially the same movements practiced in training method A, let your opponent attack you. Don't use your arms; place both hands behind your head. As you gradually get used to this, you can let your opponent's punch come quite close to your body before executing a very rapid *tai-sabaki*.

Changing direction swiftly

Pivoting must be done smoothly, with no hesitation, and the rotation of the hips must be sharp. Otherwise, the attack cannot be avoided. Speed should be at a maximum from the very beginning of the movement.

Hips on an even keel

As always, the height of the hips must be unchanged, with neither hip rising nor falling.

Sole of the foot floating

Movement is centered on the pivot leg. The sole must provide a firm base. The foot must not float or be wobbly.

Timing late

If the technique is executed after the direction is changed, timing is wrong. Execution must be simultaneous with the change in direction.

Belgium, 1976

Mediterranean Tournament, Italy, 1976

4
KEY POINTS

COORDINATION

Elbows, Knees and Shoulders

Though the techniques of karate-dō are almost limitless in number, broad classifications can be made on the basis of how the elbows and knees are used.

The elbow is straightened in order to punch (*tsuki*), thereby transmitting the power that comes from rotating the hips to the shoulder, arm and fist.

The snap of the elbow is used to strike (*uchi*), the circular movement of the arm being centered on the elbow. In the case of the back-fist strike (*uraken-uchi*), the power from the elbow is transmitted in the direction the fist travels.

The knee is straightened for the thrust kick (*kekomi*). The snap of the knee is used for the snap kick (*keage*). In the case of the thrust kick, power is applied in the direction in which the knee is straightened. In the snap kick, the power from the knee travels in an arc to the ball of the foot.

The shoulders must always be kept low—at the beginning of a technique, during its execution and even after it is ended. If the shoulders rise, it indicates that they are tense, which makes smooth movement impossible. The muscles in the side of the body will soften, and power cannot be concentrated.

When one is preoccupied with the execution of a technique, the shoulders will always rise. Instead of thinking about the technique, think of keeping the shoulders low.

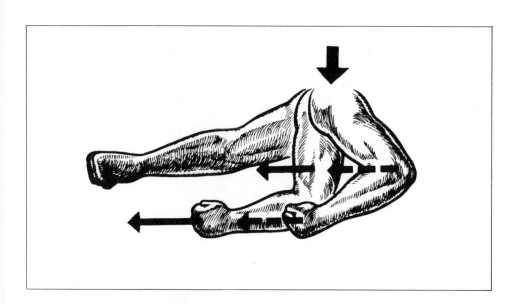

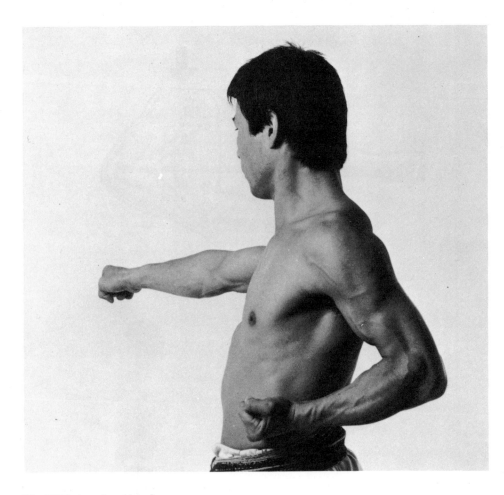

The Withdrawing Hand

The withdrawing hand (*hiki-te*) leads the rotation of the hips. When executing a technique, the withdrawing hand must move strongly, quickly and sufficiently. If not, the technique will not reach its maximum effectiveness. Another important point is that both arms must move at exactly the same time.

If a technique is being executed with the right hand, it is usual for the left elbow to be drawn straight back. However, when blocking in the half-front-facing position, it is better if the elbow comes back somewhat in the direction of the spine, rather than straight back.

When striking in a wide arc, the withdrawing arm should also describe a wide arc. In other words, if the technique is executed in a straight line, the other arm withdraws in a straight line. If the technique is arclike, the other arm travels in an arc.

It is not too much to say that excellent techniques are born from a strong, fast withdrawing arm.

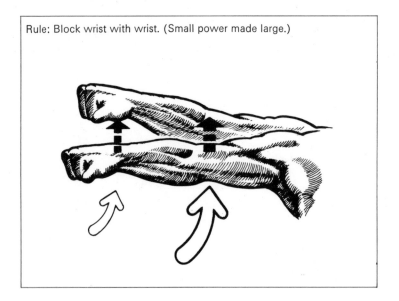

Rule: Block wrist with wrist. (Small power made large.)

Using the Wrist

When punching or blocking, the wrist is always kept firm and straight. In striking, it is usually kept straight, with some exceptions. However, in the back-fist strike, if the snap of the elbow is augmented by the snap of the wrist, the effect will be greater.

In striking with the heel of the palm (*teishō-uchi*), the bear hand (*kumade-uchi*) or the ox jaw hand (*seiryūtō-uchi*), the wrist must be fully bent and strong. This is also true when pulling the opponent toward you or when pulling him down.

The best way to block is to use your wrist against your opponent's arm or wrist. By applying relatively weak power to a specific point, the power can be amplified. This also opens up the possibility of grabbing your opponent's wrist and unbalancing him. This can be followed by a counterattack.

Strengthen your wrists through practice, for a sharp block to the opponent's arm will discourage him from further attack.

Not blocking with the wrist has these disadvantages:

Upper level: Your elbow will rise and the muscles in the side of the body will weaken.

Middle level: The block will be too high, and the blow will come under the block.

Lower level: The torso will lean forward.

Make it a motto to block with the wrist.

Ankle of supporting leg

Using the Ankles

Taking advantage of the springlike power of the ankles makes it possible to move the hips forward naturally and with great speed. The ankles also play a part in keeping the hips on an even keel and in keeping the heel of the supporting leg from floating. The ankles are important in many techniques.

In the lunge punch (*oi-zuki*), where quick body movement is necessary, the ankle of the supporting leg is important, of course. The other ankle is no less important. In the left front stance, the back leg is thrust against the floor. If at the same time, one consciously bends the ankle of the front leg sharply and strongly, the hips will be thrust forward naturally. The knee of the front leg should also be bent deeply and then brought back strongly, thus contributing to the rapid thrusting forward of the hips. The right leg slides forward quickly and smoothly, the knee is bent, and the position is that of the right lunge punch.

A front kick (*mae-geri*) from a front stance is similar to this, the knee and ankle of the front leg being suddenly bent and the center of gravity being shifted forward. The kicking leg, of course, is lifted high, and the snap of the knee is used.

To say that the effectiveness of the kick depends on the balance at the time the knee is raised and the firmness of the ankle of the supporting leg is no exaggeration. In both the lunge punch and front kick, proper use of the ankles makes for natural, automatic and rapid forward movement of the hips, thus for a technique of maximum speed and effectiveness.

Ankle of supporting leg

Ankle of kicking leg

Position of the Elbow

The closer the elbow is to the side of the chest (*wakibara*), the greater is the power that will be delivered to the attacking arm.

In punching, not only should the shoulders not rise but the elbows should not escape from the side of the body. An attack can then be made within a certain range, which will be decided largely by the necessity of keeping the side of the body tight.

In blocking, the position of the elbow should be about the width of one fist in front of the body and aligned with the side of the body. When blocking to the side, however, the elbow should be right next to the side of the body.

Age-uke   Rising Block

The elbow should be raised to the height of the ear and should be close to it. Keep the side of the body tight.

Chūdan Ude Uke   Forearm Block against Body Attack

Ideally, the elbow should be the width of one fist in front of the side of the body. The maximum allowable distance is the width of two fists. Anything greater than this will result in weakness in the side of the body. The elbow should not go outward beyond the side of the body, and the forearm should point toward the side of the body.

Chūdan Shutō Uke   Sword Hand Block against Body Attack

The position of the elbow is the same as in the forearm block against body attack.

Kagi-zuki   Hook Punch
Mizu-nagare Kamae   Flowing Water Position

The forearm is fifteen to eighteen centimeters in front of the solar plexus and parallel to it. Take care that the fist does not go too far to the opposite side. The forearm slants slightly downward. From this position, apply the springlike power of the shoulder and elbow.

Forearm block against body attack

Rising block

Sword hand block against body attack

Hook punch

91

Keeping the elbow in the same position, practice the following sequence:

Chūdan soto-uke
Gedan-barai
Chūdan uchi-uke
Age-uke

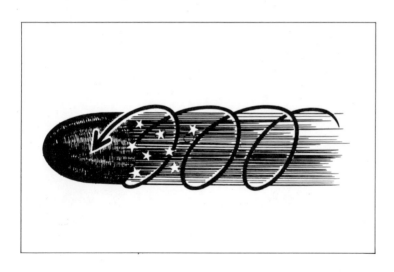

Twisting the Forearm

The twisting of the forearm bears a direct relation to maximizing the effectiveness of a technique.

In punching, the forearm should be thrust straight out to the heart of the target. This is just like thrusting a spear; in both cases, the twisting motion contributes to setting a true course. The principle is the same as that of rifling in a gun barrel. Without the rifling, the bullet would tumble end over end and veer from its course. Because of the rifling, the bullet spins and travels a true course.

Although a forearm that is not twisted can travel as fast as one that is twisted, the twisting motion gives better direction and greater impact on the target. Twisting the forearm concentrates power and amplifies it. This is true because the twisting causes an instantaneous tensing of all the muscles involved in the technique. The karate masters of old knew of this and were able to make their fists penetrate the opponent's skin and damage internal organs.

Timing: In punching, the twisting of the forearm begins when the elbow leaves the hip and ends when the fist meets the target. Karateka of advanced ranks will begin the twisting motion an instant before the fist reaches the target. This is very effective, but those who have not reached a high level of proficiency will not find it so, because their wrists will slide off target, negating the effect.

Muhammad Ali's punch. Good timing.

Timing

As in any sport, timing in karate-dō is one of the most critical factors. Whether it is a decisive technique—punching or kicking—or blocking or counterattacking, and no matter how strong or accurate the technique may be otherwise, timing must be precise. Being the least bit early or the least bit late is nothing but a mistake.

Starting the movement at the proper time is also important. In baseball and golf, the batter or golfer has his backswing. But in karate-dō, where victory or defeat is decided in no time at all, the equivalent of a backswing is simply impermissible. Late timing can be fatal. Therefore, successful techniques come from having the fist ready and the feet in position, and these must be appropriate to the situation.

The moment a technique is completed, you should take a new stance, one in which you can have confidence that you are ready to deliver the next technique to the next target immediately. In this respect, it is ideal if you can selectively maintain muscles in the appropriate state of tension.

Under all circumstances in karate, space and time have limits. If these are ignored, good timing is impossible. Careful attention must be given to the speed of the opponent's attack and to the distance between you and him, i.e., to distancing (*maai*). This is the most important point in timing.

Balance is a matter of dynamics, of moving the body, shifting the center of gravity. Important in all sports, good balance depends on stability. To achieve good stability, both feet should be firmly planted and the area they outline should be as large as possible. Then arms and legs should move in coordination with the shifting of the center of gravity, which, ideally, should not go outside the base area of the feet.

In punching or striking, the center of gravity is lowered and is located over the center of the base area described by the feet. Then the movement of all parts of the body can be regulated and power can be applied to the target. As the center of gravity moves toward the edge of the base area, balance weakens. If the center of gravity goes outside the base area, the harmony of the body is broken and balance lost.

Without balance, no technique can be effective, nor can a position be taken for the next technique. And defense against attack becomes impossible.

Leg techniques, of course, present the biggest challenge to maintaining stability and balance, so special care must be taken to keep the center of gravity from going outside the base area. However, it is not unusual for the center of gravity to go outside the area of the single supporting foot. When this happens to a slight extent, the sense organs, nerves and muscles act automatically to bring the body back and balance can be maintained, though only by a narrow margin.

The lower the center of gravity, the greater the stability. In kicking, however, bending the knee of the supporting leg too much and lowering the hips too far will make a sharp and effective kick impossible. Except for the special case of avoiding an upper level attack by shrinking the body, it is better not to bend the knees anymore than necessary. It should also be noted that if the knee is bent deeply when kicking, the heel will rise, because the center of gravity will move in the direction of the kick. When the center of gravity does shift, a new base area must be established immediately, so after a kick, the kicking foot is brought down in front of the supporting foot and a front stance, or other stance, is taken in preparation for the next technique.

Raising the heel when kicking is not only unstable but also tenses muscles unnecessarily and causes fatigue. The sole of the supporting foot must be completely in firm contact with the floor.

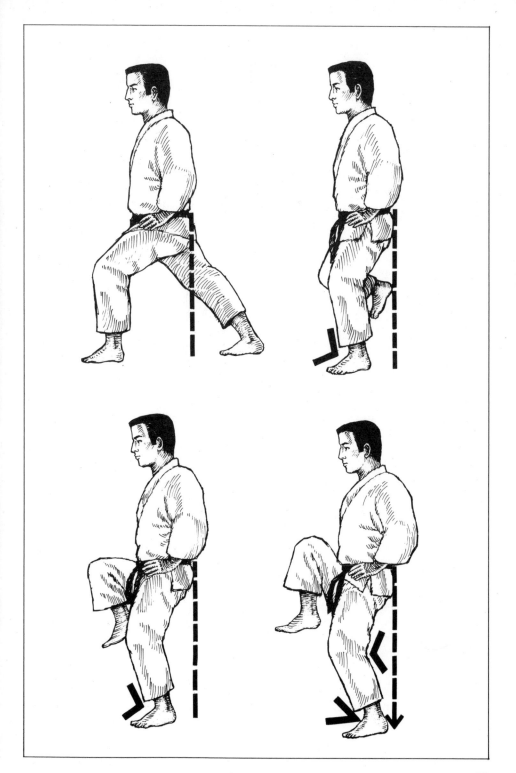

Front kick

A. Best balance, center of gravity over sole
B. Maintaining balance though center of gravity moves outside base area of foot
C. Difficult to maintain balance if center of gravity moves far outside base area of foot

Range

It is important to know your own limits. This is an aspect of distancing. Trying to increase one's range beyond natural limits leads to instability and gives the opponent an opening.

In punching and striking, find and maintain the equilibrium between range and accuracy. The upper body must confront the target in a natural way up till the final moment, so the power of the shoulders and elbows can reach the maximum.

Stance and Striking Range

The range within which one can effectively punch or strike varies according to the distance between the feet and the height of the hips. Leaning forward does not increase range at all, but it does upset balance. In diagrams 1, 2 and 3, the back foot is in the same position. According to whether the target is nearer or farther away, range can be controlled by regulating the height of the hips and the position of the other foot.

Kicking Range

Not only must the upper body be straight, it must ride on the hips. Leaning forward does not increase range. A bent back or too deep bending of the supporting knee will result in a weak technique or a successful attack by the opponent.

Result of not using the hips when kicking

Stance and striking range

Keep head steady.

Keeping the Head Steady

The head should not move unnecessarily; as much as possible, it should be kept in the same position. This is true in all sports and martial arts.

If the neck is not kept in place, or the head lowers or shakes from side to side, or, especially, if the chin rises, the technique will not be accurate and concentration of power and balance will be adversely affected. This is particularly true when kicking.

During a match, even slight errors in timing or balance result in defeat. This is observed often.

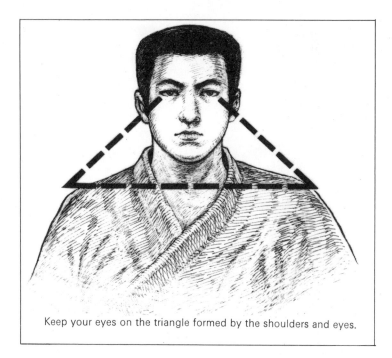

Keep your eyes on the triangle formed by the shoulders and eyes.

The Eyes

The way one's eyes look is a matter of great importance. In the martial eyes, it is said that the eyes are life. Whatever is in one's heart will appear in his eyes. Weak points will immediately be seen by the opponent. A fierce fighting spirit manifested in piercing eyes will make the opponent recoil from you.

One of the lessons of kendō is never to take your eyes off your opponent's eyes. This applies in karate-dō as well. The specific area to be watched is the triangle formed by the eyes and the two shoulders. By concentrating the eyes on this area, it is possible to know beforehand what the opponent's next move will be. Do not drop your eyes, whether taking a position or executing a technique.

Remember, too, that closing the eyes when executing a technique is inexcusable. You will not perceive the speed of your opponent's movement nor changes in movement. After all, techniques can have a speed of as much as thirteen or fourteen meters per second.

I myself have had the experience of being hit (in the forehead) simply because the timing of my block was off by a fraction of a second. This happened during a photographing session when the strobe was flashing at one-thousandth of a second and was due to my having blinked.

Bad habits should be corrected completely.

Correct Route in Punching

A punch cannot be effective unless the route it travels is correct. In the case of the straight punch (*choku-zuki*), the correct route is a straight line between the fist in its position of readiness and the target, which is the shortest possible distance. To accomplish this, the elbow of the punching arm should lightly brush the side of the body and the forearm should twist inward. Power traveling in a direct, straight line does not change direction even after hitting the target, and this has great meaning in timing. (See page 95.)

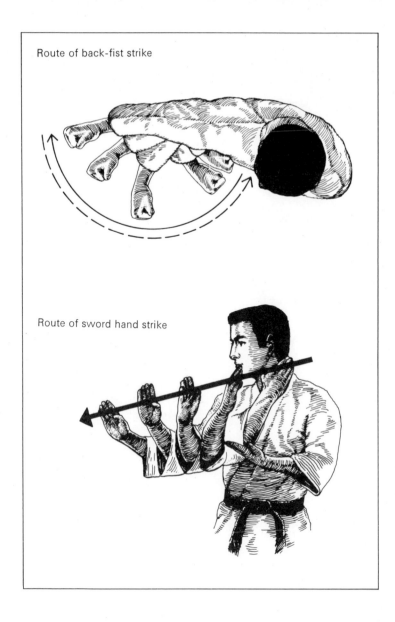

Route of back-fist strike

Route of sword hand strike

In Striking

The fist must be tightly clenched, the sword hand firmly tightened. Quickly and fully apply the spring and snap of the elbow.

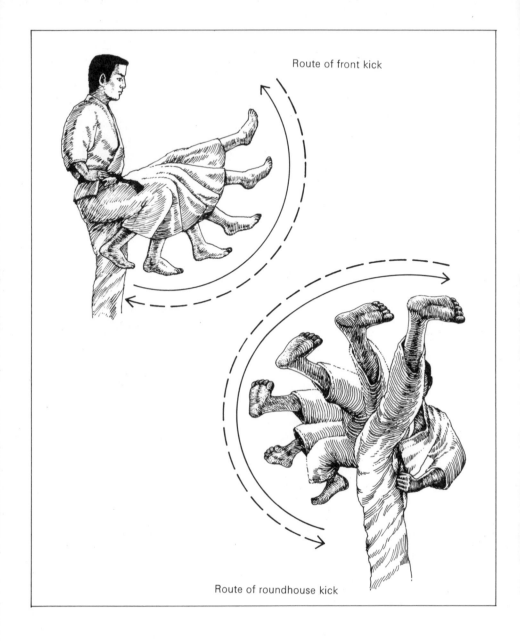

Route of front kick

Route of roundhouse kick

In Kicking

An effective true kick is born from the correct use of the snap or the straightening of the knee.

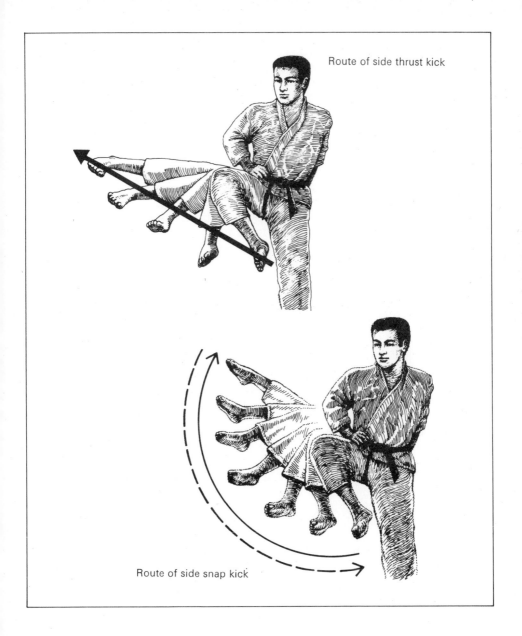

Route of side thrust kick

Route of side snap kick

In Blocking

To block, it is necessary to first judge the course of the attacking arm or leg accurately, then block in the appropriate direction. Basically:

1. Thrust upward against an upper level attack.

2. Block a middle level attack to the side, either inside outward or outside inward.

3. Block a punch or kick to the lower level diagonally downward.

In the Upper Block against Head Attack

1. Raise the left forearm from below the right elbow, keeping it to the outer side and bring it to the forehead. The path of the left arm is somewhat like an arc but slightly pointed. It is possible to do this in a straight line, but only if one is stronger or more experienced than his opponent.

2. Open the left fist and bring the thumb side of the palm along the bridge of the nose. At the same time, raise the right forearm from the hip, without letting the elbow go outward. The arms cross in front of the jaw to keep the block on the correct route. Block diagonally upward with the right forearm.

In the Forearm Block against Body Attack

Outside inward
From a position by the right ear, the right fist sweeps downward and to the left side. Block in front of the chin. The course of the block is a semicircle.

Inside outward
From a position by the right side, the left arm goes outside the withdrawing arm, the blocking arm rising with the elbow as the pivot. Block in front of the jaw. For a left arm block, rotate the hips strongly to the right and withdraw the right arm strongly.

In the Downward Block

From a position near the right ear, the left fist sweeps diagonally downward with the straightening of the elbow. Block with the wrist (palm downward) above the left kneecap (about fifteen centimeters).

In the Sword Hand Block against Body Attack

From a position near the left ear, the right sword hand cuts diagonally downward, with the elbow still bent, striking and blocking.

Route of downward block

Route of forearm block
against body attack

Route of upper block against head attack

Speed

In a decisive technique (*kime-waza*), there is power that is instantaneous and formidable. The basic techniques of karate are influenced to a very great extent by speed. It may be a bit of an exaggeration to say that in training in techniques, speed is first in importance and second in importance, but it is no exaggeration to say that the objective of basic training is maximizing speed.

Since the body is organized in three basic parts, power comes from increasing speed in all of them. If the muscles involved are contracted as fast as possible, then the power that reaches the hand in punching or the foot in kicking will reach its maximum level. In punching, in order to take advantage of the pairing of forces that comes from withdrawing the other arm, it must be withdrawn as fast as possible.

Speed is dependent, for one thing, on muscular control. When certain muscles contract, other muscles expand. In punching, for example, the triceps expand while the biceps strongly contract. If proper coordination between the expansion and contraction is lacking, then the movement of the arm will not be smooth and an effective punching technique is not possible.

Beginners have a tendency to use unnecessary muscles. They should accept guidance and, according to their training, learn to consciously control their muscles.

108

Generally speaking, the meaning of *decisive technique* is to attack the selected target in an instant with power at its maximum limit.

In punching, start from the correct position and keep all unnecessary power out of the hand and arm. Then from a smooth and speedy start, concentrate the power of the whole body harmoniously and instantaneously. The great power of the hips is concentrated and transmitted like chain lightning through the chest, shoulder, upper arm and forearm to the attacking surface of the fist.

Tensing the muscles of the front and sides of the abdomen solidly links the pelvis and the shoulders. A stable pelvis and the complementary muscle groups of the thigh working together contribute to strong movements and a stable stance. This strong foundation gives support and makes it possible for the power of the hips to be transmitted to the arm. The triceps, used in raising the arm, and the forearm muscles are tensed, while the muscles around the armpit are relaxed. If these are not relaxed, the fist will rebound from the target.

Hips, chest, shoulder, arm, wrist and fist—all must be firmly linked together, and all muscles must function fully. But if the shoulder is raised when punching, or leads the movement of the body, the muscles around the armpit will not work properly, no matter how much the arm muscles are contracted. Then the impact will probably cause the fist to rebound from the target.

What is true in the case of punching is also true of striking and kicking.

Do not use power unnecessarily. It should reach the maximum level at the time of impact and return immediately to zero. Relaxing power does not mean relaxing alertness. Always relax power that is not needed, but be alert and ready to apply all the power of your body and fighting spirit the instant it is called for.

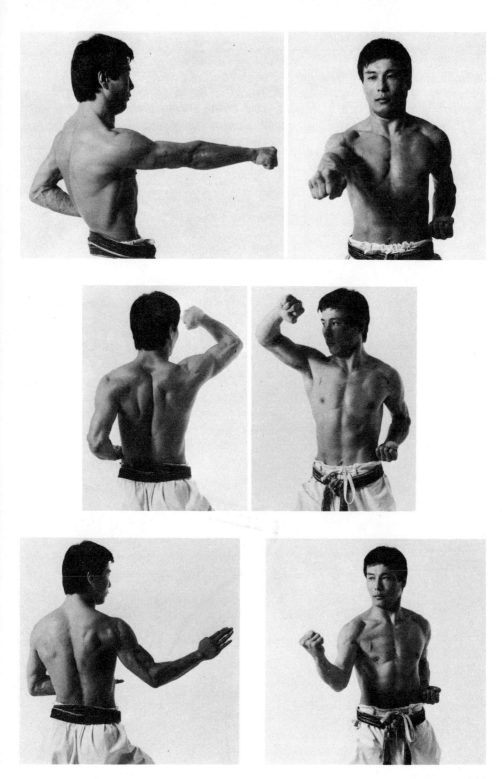

BLOCKING, PUNCHING, STRIKING, KICKING

BLOCKING

The difficulty of defending oneself by blocking should never be underestimated. What is your opponent's target? What is his intention? Judging the nature of the attack is in itself very difficult, but if you do no more than this, sooner or later you will be caught in a trap, no matter how good you become. What is necessary is to coolly assess the attack, take care of your own body in an advantageous way, and be prepared for any eventuality.

The basically important possibilities in blocking are:

1. Block strongly. This will have a chilling effect on the adversary's enthusiasm. To put it another way, let the block be an attack.

2. Block lightly to bring the opponent under control.

3. Go from block to attack instantaneously. Or make the block itself into an attack.

4. Use the block to upset your opponent.

5. Suppress the attack by blocking before the attack really gets under way.

6. Stay at a safe distance and wait for the opportunity to counterattack.

The biggest difference between karate and other sports is that one must be able to block foot and leg techniques as well as hand and arm techniques. Therefore, the feet and legs are also used to block, and karate is unique in this respect.

Overblocking

It is not uncommon to see beginners waving their arms about instead of blocking. A block is a block only when the position is correct. Do not overblock.

Overblocking makes the sides of the body weak and adversely affects balance. It is then impossible to execute a technique. It also disrupts the ability to tense various muscle groups and their harmonious functioning. Then even a weak attack cannot be handled.

Incorrect Blocking

Arm away from the body

Elbow too high

Elbow too high

Too low

Elbow out of position

Block on too small a scale

Block is too high.

Hips not turning

Blocking as Decisive Technique

As mentioned before, a blocking technique, depending on how it is used, may become a decisive technique. This can be seen often in karate-dō, though not in other martial arts. A technique that starts as a block and continues without stopping to become a decisive one is probably unique to karate.

Age-uke   *Rising Block*

The rising block can be turned into an attack by lowering the hips slightly and letting the upper body go very slightly forward. Then step forward under the attacking arm and use the block to simultaneously attack the chin or the point below the nose with the bottom of the fist, and the armpit with the elbow.

Another way is to follow up the block by grasping the opponent's wrist with the blocking hand and strongly striking his elbow with the other hand.

Ude Uke   *Forearm Block*
Shutō Uke   *Sword Hand Block*

As the opponent moves to attack, step forward. This requires good timing. While stepping forward, sweep widely with the fist or sword hand, quickly striking the point below the nose with the fist, or the eyes with the sword hand, before your opponent's blow connects.

If a blow is directed to your face, bring your elbow a little to the side and push the attacking arm from inside outward. Then attack his face.

118

Stamping kick–rising block

Hiji suri-uke Sliding elbow block (block-punch)

Hiji suri-uke Sliding elbow block (block-punch)

Stamping kick–sword hand block

Basic Training in Blocking

Facing your partner at a distance close enough to touch him, practice the following, then switch roles.

A		B
Right punch to face	→	Right rising block
Left rising block	←	Left punch to face
Right punch to body	→	Right forearm block, outside inward
Left forearm block, outside inward	←	Left punch to body
Right punch to lower level	→	Right downward block
Left downward block	←	Left punch to lower level

A		B
Right punch to face	→	Left rising block
Left rising block	←	Right punch to face
Right punch to body	→	Left forearm block, outside inward
Left forearm block, outside inward	←	Right punch to body
Right punch to lower level	→	Left downward block
Left downward block	←	Right punch to lower level

Practice forearm blocks both inside outward and outside inward. Practice slowly at first, increasing speed and power gradually.

PUNCHING

Gyaku-zuki   *Reverse Punch*

Lower the hips and rotate them with good timing, utilizing fully the power that comes from straightening the back leg and driving it into the floor. The stance must be stable, and the hips always on an even keel. The pelvis, and hence the center of gravity, shifts slightly forward. A punch delivered with the hips even a little to the rear will not be effective. The power transmitted from the leg and hips to the chest, shoulders and arm accelerates, but for this to be true, the body and limbs must be solidly joined together, like an iron rod or a steel plate. This depends on the muscles working in harmony and tensing powerfully at the same instant.

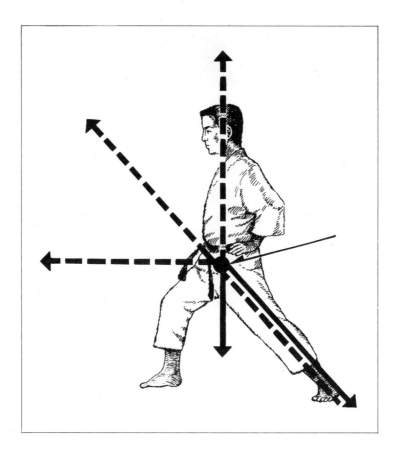

Oi-zuki   Lunge Punch

From the front stance (or natural position), advance the rear leg well forward into another front stance, simultaneously attacking with the fore-fist to the head or chest. Advance quickly, using the power from the supporting leg. If this is not done, the advancing leg may be swept by the opponent. Therefore, take care to slide the foot quickly and easily without raising the heel. The hips, carrying the center of gravity, must move directly toward the target and directly away from the pivot foot. Because the center of gravity moves a fairly long distance, this is a very powerful punch.

Nagashi-zuki   Flowing Punch

As with the lunge punch, the movement of the body makes this punch strong. It can be delivered from the half-front-facing position or while moving diagonally forward or backward. This is very effective for a blocking-counterattack, because the hips are used while moving diagonally.

Kizami-zuki   *Jab*

   This is a variation of the lunge punch. Since the pivot leg does not move, power comes from the hip rotation and the downward thrusting of the rear leg. It can be delivered either without shifting the center of gravity or when moving the hips forward. Though it can be used decisively, the jab is more often an intermediate tactic to be followed immediately by a lunge punch or reverse punch with the other fist.

STRIKING

Snap in Striking Techniques

The use of snap is nowhere more important than in striking techniques. The snap and springlike power of the elbow can be applied to the front, sides, back, upward or downward, while turning to one side, to the rear or diagonally.

The following points are important:

1. The forearm must be extended quickly in an arc-shaped motion centered on the elbow. No effect can be expected if there is tension in the elbow.

2. If the shoulders are not relaxed and the fist or sword hand not tensed fully, good snap is impossible. Always relax all unnecessary tension.

3. The bigger the arc, the more effective the power. Straighten the elbow to the fullest extent. It is not a good idea to withdraw the forearm unless the elbow has been straightened to the fullest extent.

4. Speed is of first importance—no speed, no effect.

5. Snap the arm outward with maximum speed and to the maximum extent using the triceps, but once this is done immediately relax the triceps. The biceps will then automatically bring the forearm back, and the snap will be complete. Practice diligently to understand how the arm muscles work.

6. The greatest effect comes when the forearm moves near the body. Twisting the forearm increases effectiveness.

 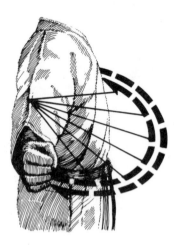

Striking with the Fist

Whether striking to the side or vertically, the snap of the elbow and wrist makes the difference.

Yoko-mawashi Uchi   **Horizontal Strike**

Extending the forearm to the side in a movement parallel to the floor and centered on the elbow is *yoko-mawashi uchi*.

Tate-mawashi Uchi   **Vertical Strike**

Extending the forearm vertically is called *tate-mawashi uchi*. The points are a relaxed elbow (no tension) and a tight fist.

Shutō Uchi   Sword Hand Strike

When striking from inside outward, the hips rotate in the opposite direction; when striking from outside inward, they rotate in the direction of the strike. Twisting the forearms is the effective way.

Uchi-mawashi   Inside Outward

Strike the target from inside outward by rotating the hips, twisting the forearm and straightening the elbow all at the same time.

Soto-mawashi   Outside Inward

Strike the target from outside inward by rotating the hips, twisting the forearm and straightening the elbow all at the same time.

Improving Elbow Techniques

Good technique comes from keeping the fist of the striking arm close to the body, drawing it straight from one nipple to the other.

Yoko Hiji-ate — Side Elbow Strike

In striking with the right elbow, slide the right fist in a straight line from the left nipple to the right nipple and twist the forearm.

Mae Hiji-ate — Forward Elbow Strike

As in punching, the fist brushes the side of the body, but unlike punching, it stays close to the body until it reaches the nipple on the opposite side. Twist the forearm in front of the chest, so the palm is downward.

Tate Hiji-ate — Upward Elbow Strike

With the elbow fully bent, bring the fist up alongside the body as far as the ear (palm inward). The elbow rises higher than this level to strike the target.

Ushiro Hiji-ate — Back Elbow Strike

Like the withdrawing arm in punching, the elbow brushes the side of the body and is then thrust strongly to the rear.

Otoshi hiji-ate — Downward Elbow Strike

The elbow is raised high and bent suddenly. Then it—and the hips as well—are brought straight down.

Mawashi Hiji-ate — Roundhouse Elbow Strike

Twist the forearm while raising the elbow and bring the right fist to the right nipple (if striking with the right arm). Then use the elbow to strike outward to a target at the side.

KICKING

Bending the Knee Correctly

Lifting the leg high and bending the knee fully is the preparatory stage in kicking. Doing this correctly, that is lightly and very quickly, helps one to maintain balance and to discover the correct route of the kick.

Since both the hip and thigh muscles necessary for this have some connection with the pelvis, the hips must be stable if the muscles are to operate fully. This in turn requires a strong abdomen.

Steadiness in the supporting leg depends on tensing the muscles of the thigh and calf and bending the knee, but only slightly. The calf should lean forward, but only slightly, and the sole must be firmly on the floor. If the knee is bent too much in an effort to keep the hips low, the muscles will not give good support and the knee and ankle will become weak, making an effective kick impossible.

The kneecap of the kicking leg should come as high as the chest, so the weight of the leg falls toward the hip.

The Spring of the Hips and Ankle

Neither the snap kick nor the thrust kick can be executed effectively using only the power of the legs. The spring of the hips and ankles must be applied, and, ideally, at the instant of kicking, the lumbar vertebrae should push forward. But the hips must come back immediately at the end of the kick. This movement of the hips and the shock of kicking has the greatest effect on the ankle of the supporting leg. The ankle thus plays the major role in maintaining balance and a stable posture. Lifting the heel or otherwise lessening contact between the sole and the floor leads to instability. The ankles, therefore must be strong, and this depends on training. Though the knee is bent slightly, its position is fixed.

Keage   *Snap Kick*

The calf leans forward slightly, the lumbar vertebrae move forward and come back, and the calf must return to its original position. These all depend on the expansion and contraction of the leg muscles.

Because the area of the supporting foot is small and the direction of the kick is usually upward, balance is the greatest problem. Moreover, there is the necessity of returning as quickly as possible to a wider stance with both feet on the floor in order to be ready for the next technique. For both of these reasons, speed is the *sine qua non* of kicking. A slow snap kick lacks power and is very unstable. With regard to speed, it can even be said that the withdrawal of the kicking leg is more than twice as important as the kick itself, or at least that is the feeling one must have.

Kekomi   *Thrust Kick*

At the moment of contact, the thigh and calf should form a nearly straight line. As in the case of the straight punch, the route should be the shortest and the straightest. It takes a lot of practice to kick in the correct way, which is to start with a light quick movement and concentrate all of the body power at the instant of contact.

The most important point in the thrust kick is distancing. When the leg is straight and power concentrated, the kick is very powerful, but if the knee is bent or the timing imprecise, the kicking leg will rebound. The negative reaction is greatest when the leg is fully bent but improperly focused. This would have a more adverse effect on balance when kicking straight to the side than when kicking diagonally downward; the greatest disruption would come when kicking upward. It will not due to forget the influence of distancing on power even for a moment.

SKELETAL MUSCLES

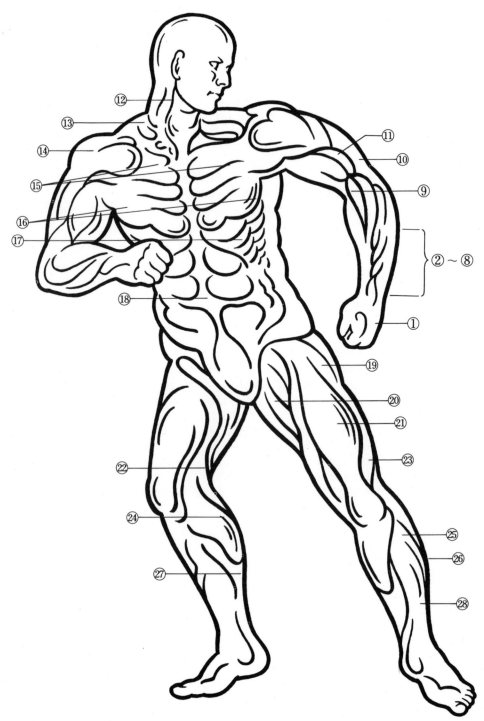

HAND
1. Interosseus

FOREARM
2. Abductor pollicis brevis
3. Palmaris longus
4. Flexor carpi radialis
5. Extensor carpi radialis brevis
6. Pronator teres
7. Extensor carpi radialis longus
8. Brachioradialis

UPPER ARM
9. Triceps
10. Brachialis
11. Biceps

SHOULDERS AND NECK
12. Sternocleidomastoideus
13. Trapezius
14. Deltoid

CHEST AND ABDOMEN
15. Pectoralis major
16. Serratus anterior
17. Obliquus abdominis externus
18. Rectus abdominis

THIGH
19. Tensor fasciae latae
20. Adductor magnus
21. Rectus femoris
22. Vastus medialis
23. Vastus lateralis

CALF
24. Gastrocnemius
25. Tibialis anterior
26. Peronaeus longus
27. Flexor digitorum longus
28. Peronaeus brevis

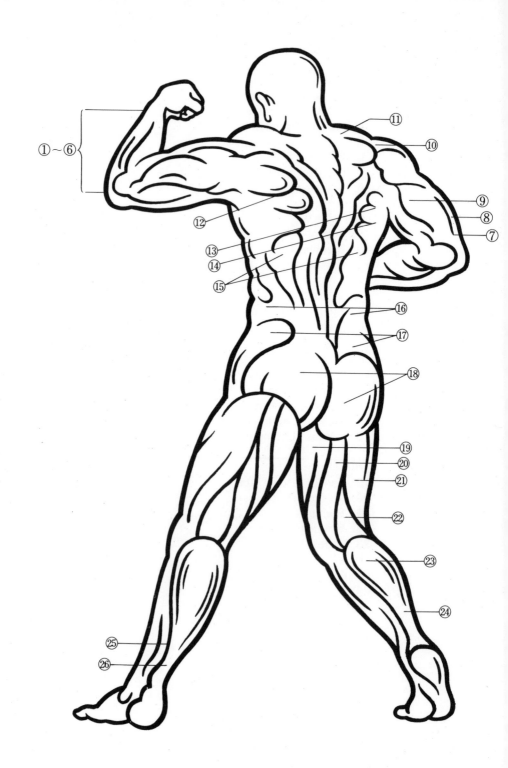

FOREARM
1. Extensor pollicis brevis
2. Flexor carpi ulnaris
3. Extensor carpi ulnaris
4. Abductor pollicis longus
5. Extensor digitorum communis
6. Anconeus

UPPER ARM
7. Brachioradialis
8. Brachialis
9. Triceps

SHOULDERS, NECK AND BACK
10. Deltoid
11. Trapezius
12. Infraspinatus
13. Teres minor
14. Teres major
15. Latissimus dorsi
16. Obliquus externus abdominis
17. Glutaeus medius

THIGH
18. Glutaeus maximus
19. Adductor magnus
20. Semitendinous
21. Biceps femoris
22. Semimembranosus

CALF
23. Gastrocnemius
24. Soleus
25. Peronaeus longus
26. Peronaeus brevis

PRACTICE SCHEDULE
FOR BASIC TECHNIQUES

First Week
PUNCHING   Natural position, open leg stance
1. Face target squarely. 2. Shortest distance. 3. Speed. 4. Concentration of power.

KICKING   Natural position, informal attention stance
1. Raise knee chest-high. 2. Use snap. 3. The importance of kicking to withdrawing the leg is in the ratio of 3 to 7. 4. Tighten ankle of supporting leg; keep knee at correct angle. 5. Bend knee of kicking leg swiftly.

Second Week
FRONT STANCE   From half-front-facing position to front-facing position; from front-facing position to half-front-facing position. (Hands on hips.)
1. Appropriate distance between feet. 2. Knee and toe of the same leg pointing in the same direction. 3. Force the knee of the front leg out strongly in the direction of the line connecting the two knees. 4. Both hips parallel to the floor.

REVERSE PUNCH   Front stance
1. Bring back withdrawing hand strongly and widely. 2. Lead hip rotation with withdrawing hand. 3. Use counter-reaction from straightening back leg.

FRONT KICK   Front Stance
1. Calf of supporting leg leans forward; thrust hips forward quickly. 2. Knee and toes of the supporting leg must point in the direction of the kick.

Third Week
LUNGE PUNCH (A)   Alternately to the left and right from natural position
1. Drive strongly with the supporting leg, use the reaction, and thrust the hips forward quickly. 2. Slide the moving leg lightly, keeping the entire sole in contact with the floor.

DOWNWARD BLOCK   Alternately to the left and right from the natural position or front stance
1. Taking the half-front-facing position, bring back the withdrawing hand completely. 2. Wide and sharp rotation of hips. 3. Bring blocking arm from above elbow swiftly; twist forearm. (Straighten elbow fully.)

Fourth Week

LUNGE-PUNCH (B)   Advance from the final position of the downward block (*gedan-gamae*).

1. Calf of supporting leg leans forward; thrust hips forward quickly. 2. Bring rear leg to front leg; shift weight to front leg. With front leg as pivot leg, step forward and thrust out hips.

STRADDLE-LEG STANCE   Left and right from natural position

1. Soles of both feet in good contact with the floor. 2. Push knee of front leg in the direction of the line connecting the two knees.

Fifth Week

SIDE SNAP KICK   Informal attention stance

1. Face to the front. 2. Raise knee high at the side of the body. 3. Use snap (centered on kneecap). Kicking leg starts and ends by the side of the knee.

RISING BLOCK   Alternately to left and right from natural position or front stance

Sixth Week

SIDE THRUST KICK   Informal attention stance

1. Kicking knee to chest level; straighten leg completely for the kick. 2. Leg travels the same route when kicking and when returning.

FOREARM BLOCK   Alternately to left and right from natural position, front stance or straddle-leg stance

1. Outside inward: elbow bent to form right angle, arclike motion to the outer side, striking block. 2. Inside outward: elbow one fist-width from side of body, fist at shoulder height, forearm moving with elbow as the pivot, striking block to the inside.

Seventh Week

BACK STANCE   Forward, backward, left and right from the natural position

1. Body weight back to front in ratio of 7 to 3. Front knee bent slightly. 3. Upper body vertically straight in half-front-facing position.

SWORD HAND BLOCK   Natural position or back stance

1. Blocking arm slashing diagonally downward from shoulder. 2. Elbow one fist-width from side of body. 3. Elbow bent in right angle.

Eighth Week

BLOCKING TO PUNCHING   Alternately to left and right from nat-

| BLOCKING TO KICKING | ural position, open-leg stance From upper, middle and lower level blocks to kicks. Alternate from front stance to back stance. |

Ninth Week

| BODY MOVEMENT | Blocking and counterattacking, forward, backward and to both sides |

1. Smooth leg movement and *tai-sabaki.* 2. Learn from experience how to move most satisfactorily. 3. Arm movement also must be smooth.

Tenth through Twelfth Weeks

| KATA | Heian 1 |

age-uke: rising block, 20, 90, 118, 141

choku-zuki: straight punch, 20, 102
chūdan shutō uke: sword hand block against body attack, 90, 106
chūdan uchi-uke: forearm block against body attack, inside outward, 22
chūdan ude uke: forearm block against body attack, 90, 106

dō: movement, activity, 60
dō-kyaku: moving leg, 60

fumidashi: 68
fumikomi: stamping kick, 60, 68

gedan barai: downward block, 22, 106
gedan-gamae: downward block position, 141
gyaku hanmi: reverse half-front-facing position, 24
gyaku kaiten: reverse rotation, 22
gyaku-zuki: reverse punch, 124, 140

hanmi: half-front-facing position, 18, 24
heisoku-dachi: informal attention stance, 30
hiji suri-uke: sliding elbow block, 120
hiki-te: withdrawing hand, 16, 84

ikken hissatsu: to kill with one blow, 11

jiku ashi: pivot leg, 60
jiyū kumite: free sparring, 10
jōdan age-uke: upper block against head attack, 106
jun kaiten: regular rotation, 20

kagi-zuki: hook punch, 20, 90
katachi: form, 56
keage: snap kick, 82, 135
kekomi: thrust kick, 82, 135
keri: kicking, 104, 132, 140, 141
kiba-dachi: straddle-leg stance, 52, 141
kime: finish, 11
kime-waza: decisive technique, 14, 108, 109
kizami-zuki: jab, 127
kōkutsu-dachi: back stance, 52, 141
kōsa-dachi: crossed-feet stance, 52
kumade-uchi: bear hand strike, 86
maai: distancing, 95
mae-geri: front kick, 88, 140
mae hiji-ate: forward elbow strike, 131
mawashi hiji-ate: roundhouse elbow strike, 131
mawashi-zuki: roundhouse punch, 20
mizu-nagare kamae: flowing water position, 90

nagashi-zuki: flowing punch, 126
neko-ashi-dachi: cat leg stance, 52

oi-zuki: lunge punch, 88, 126, 140
otoshi hiji-ate: downward elbow strike, 131

sei: tranquillity, inactivity, 60
seiryūtō-uchi: ox-jaw hand strike, 86
shutō uchi: sword hand strike; *uchi-mawashi,* inside outward, 130: *soto-mawashi,* 130
shutō uke: sword hand block, 22, 118, 141
soto-uke: block from outside inward, 20
sun-dome: arresting a technique, 11

143